thon craigheau

STUART
CROFT
FOUNDATION

thomson & craighead

with essays by michael archer and julian stallabrass

film and video umbrella

minigraph 7

First published 2005 by Film and Video Umbrella
52 Bermondsey Street London SE1 3UD
Tel: 020 7407 7755
Fax: 020 7407 7766
HTTP://www.fvumbrella.com

film and video umbrella

This publication was supported by a Grants for Arts award from
Arts Council England, London, and received additional support
from CARTE, University of Westminster.

ISBN 1 90427 017 4

Edited by Steven Bode and Nina Ernst
Design by Claudia Schenk
Printed and bound at Graphicom, Italy

British Library Cataloguing in Publication Data: a CIP record for this
publication is available from the British Library

contents

er... stolen

michael archer

It's a simple computer game. There's a fleet of gunships that you can use to fire at a target that is, virus-like, bleeding destructive depth charges down the screen. A quartet of protective blocks can be hidden behind until such time as they, too, are destroyed. The format is familiar from early video games such as 'Space Invaders', but with a twist: instead of firing at the usual assortment of military hardware the target at which you aim is a text. Jon Thomson and Alison Craighead's *Triggerhappy* presents the player with a dilemma — whether to go for maximum obliteration or to pause in order to read the words before they dissolve. The text is a quotation from Michel Foucault's essay, 'What is an Author?', which, together with Roland Barthes' 'The Death of the Author', remains a key exploration of the degree to which the coherent identity of the writer is an effect, rather than the origin, of a text. Foucault opens by observing two characteristics of writing: that it creates a space into which the (writing) subject constantly disappears, and that it is a way of warding off death. And he ends with a host of questions:

'What are the modes of existence of this discourse? Where has it been used, how can it circulate, and who can appropriate it for himself? What are the places in it where there is room for possible subjects? Who can assume these various subject-functions?' And behind all these questions, we would hear hardly anything but the stirring of an indifference: 'What difference does it make who is speaking?'[1]

What is to be done? Should one kill these words or read them? And is to make that choice tantamount to choosing between practice and theory, between doing something and thinking about what you're doing? Thomson and Craighead's work gives us the choice, and at the same time exposes that choice as less than straightforward: to choose either option is to demonstrate a mode of existence; to use the text, to appropriate it for oneself, and to find a place for oneself as subject within it.

And within the ambiguities put into play by the work one can discern a further problem: what does it mean, in this context, in connection with this technology, to exhibit the rapt attentiveness of the trigger-happy? Timothy Allen Jackson, in considering the nature of a 'digital aesthetic', turns to *picnolepsis* – Paul Virilio's term for the frequent, often unremarked dissociation of the mind's conscious thought processes from the body's sensorimotor functioning – in his attempt to analyse what is going on in such cases. It is this kind of dissociation, he says, that we exhibit over sustained periods when we are absorbed in a computer game. But while this may suggest that we are not particularly aware of the physical state of our bodies during such times, we are 'still actively constructing meaning' in such circumstances.[2] The player of computer games, in other words, is finding rather than losing him- or herself. *Triggerhappy* presents us with the similar situation, but at one remove. Rather than a mere 'finding' or 'losing' of oneself, it interrogates in what such discovery or loss might consist. Who is found, and where?

'Is anybody there?' — a direct and straightforward question that, in some ways, has become the key enquiry following the appearance and development of internet technology. Under the guise of a polite request designed, perhaps, to initiate a dialogue, it presents all of our fears about dissolution of identity and loss of place, and leads our thoughts beyond that to the dread of non-being. It is a familiar question, too – the perennial precursor to countless ghost and horror stories – yet for all its clichéd obviousness it finds new purchase when used as the term for a Google search by Thomson and Craighead. The fact that the results of this search were printed on to Egyptian cotton tea towels and offered for sale through the artists' online retail outlet, *dot-store*, only adds to the conflicting qualities of levity and profundity in the query. Is there any 'body' to be encountered anywhere within the vast hyperspatial domain of the web? And, if there is, from what possible 'there' could we understand any response to the query to have come?

Everyday conversation and media discussion on the topic of digital technology is subject to two recurrent themes — those of immersion and immateriality. The idea of immersion is a powerful one and is encountered frequently in writing on internet use. Instead of accessing the net in order to retrieve information, much as one might use a library to find a book, we are said to experience ourselves as being immersed in it or to be caught within its structure. This experience is a spatial one, the bits of information and the various possible linkages between them that we encounter on our net-based adventures constituting a sort of electromagnetic architecture, a virtual environment that invites a qualitatively new kind of habitation.[3] At the same time arguments about and analyses of digital technology seem to push us inexorably toward acceptance of the fact that the things of the world are becoming separated into their constituent parts. The material from which an object is made is detached from knowledge of the form that material takes, since form is, according to this view, information, and information can be represented digitally. A communication, no longer ink distributed in certain configurations across the surface of a piece of paper in the form of a letter, is really now only a package of information that can be sent from one computer terminal to another, or from a terminal to a fax machine, or to a printer, or to a mobile phone, or a palm pilot, or whatever. And that information can be displayed on a screen, or on some other piece of paper, or through speakers. This mutability and mobility gives rise to the mistaken notion that it makes sense to think in terms of a kind of disembodiment. William J. Mitchell, for example, talks of a process in which dematerialisation is followed by materialisation: 'You separate an object's form from its material, transmit the dematerialised form, and eventually re-embody the form with new but indistinguishable material. You dematerialise, then re-materialise. You keep the bits constant, but substitute new atoms.' But this, as Mitchell realises, is only the beginning. There need, in fact, be no original embodiment to act as model since the information file can be used to generate any number of instances in a wide variety of materials and a range of sizes.[4]

One of the effects of viewing the digital file/material substrate relationship in this way is to reinforce the old form/content view of the work of art. And here dematerialisation comes together with the idea of immersion, because what gets immersed in netspace is a consciousness conceived as separable from the body within which it resides. In a simple, not to say fatuous comparison, the mind/body split is rendered equivalent to the form/content distinction. It is an equivalence thrown into serious question, if not rendered irrelevant, by Alison Craighead's conviction that what she and Jon Thomson are exploring through their practice is the idea of information as material. Far from thinking of the words, images and sounds encountered on a web surf as immaterial, phantasmatic effects of the system, they confront the fact not only that they are open to manipulation and organisation, but also that such engagement is rooted in and bears upon the physical and the real.

Their development of what they call 'template cinema' is a case in point. The first instance of this was the group of works called *Short Films About Flying*. Each film, anachronistically modelled on silent movies, is built from the same basic set of parts: a visual sequence punctuated by intertitles carrying a written narrative is augmented by a musical accompaniment. The online feed from a camera on the perimeter of Boston's Logan Airport provides the visuals, a randomly selected music radio station gives us a soundtrack, and the story is generated from successive results of Google searches alternatively using the terms 'He said', and 'She said'. These last elements are on the whole found in blogs, since, as Craighead observes, online diaries are packed with narratives that 'lend themselves to being er… stolen'.[5] Naturally, the films can be downloaded and stored for off-line viewing, but in the first instance they are sourced and generated online by means of Thomson and Craighead's template program. Acknowledging that there is a specific technological environment both within which they are realised, and through which they are made accessible, is a quality net-based art such as this shares with a number of precursors — for example, the photograms of Moholy-Nagy and Man Ray, much work in sound, and even the telephone poetry of Bryon Gysin. The technology is not used merely as a device to record or represent a reality that exists elsewhere; it is, rather, embraced as an extension to, and qualifier of, one's total spatial possibilities. It is only within this space that such material fragments can be handled and placed in relation to one another. Thomson describes the experience by likening the web to a piece of string in which he and Craighead are tying a number of knots. The centrally-placed viewer is then able to draw relationships between these otherwise unrelated nodes.[6]

Thomson and Craighead's interest in data as material, and the enquiry their work conducts into the modalities of that materiality, stands against the romantic, would-be revolutionary view of the internet that David Sanford Horner has referred to as *cyber-idealism*. Horner is sceptical of much of the emancipatory talk inspired by internet and virtual technologies. His doubt stems from the degree to which approbation of the freedoms to be discovered online – the freedom to associate, the freedom of/from identity, the freedom, ultimately, to escape the consequences of one's actions – rests upon models of human interaction derived from science fiction and fantasy. Horner wants to draw a distinct line between fact and fiction, between the way things are and the way we might be tempted to imagine them becoming, somehow and at some unspecified future moment.[7] The problem with such a view, as Thomson and Craighead reveal to us, is that this line between what is and what might be, is not always so easy to discern. You could hit a page recently, for example, and read this:

> A videotape posted on an Islamist website apparently shows
> two men standing on a sidewalk – blindfolded, with their
> hands bound behind their backs – in front of a banner with
> the name 'al Qaeda in Iraq' in Arabic. Minutes later, the men
> were beheaded as punishment for delivering food to a U.S.
> military base.

If you had arrived at that page via a certain route, your reading of these words could have been done to a musical accompaniment. Dramatic, perhaps, in keeping with the impact of the story, or contemplative, as an inducement to consider the implications of the event, or melancholic, as an adjunct to a realisation of humankind's unending inhumanity, or jubilant, in celebration of another blow against the tyranny of the oppressor, or... or... There is death, which is final and incontrovertible, and around this death is a penumbra of assumption and interpretation, of varying points of view and the judgements consequent upon their associated systems of values. The news story was published by CNN on their website, and the means of adding the musical accompaniment via a linked site constructed by

Thomson and Craighead. *CNN Interactive just got more interactive* offers the reader a varied menu of musical styles. Choosing from this provides a soundtrack of generic, manufactured music of the required sort to colour one's reading of the news. Where does the analysis of the news end; how does the necessary and inescapable task of imposing a narrative on the world by excerpting events from the daily flow and framing them for easier assimilation mesh with the equally strong narrativising tendencies of the assimilators? How, in other words, can that line between fact and fiction be held when the fictionalising which is a part of our comprehension of the world guides and informs any and every practical decision that is subsequently taken? A more recent engagement with online news sites is *Decorative Newsfeeds*, in which stories from the BBC website are fed through a programme that turns them into swirling, looping strings of text. Projected onto both sides of a screen suspended in the middle of the room, these brief synopses of current events become active presences, knotting and unravelling as they slither around the space before one's eyes.

In both its title and its form *Decorative Newsfeeds* recognises that to experience the net is to experience a flow of signals, impulses or information that, while being transient and fugitive, is nonetheless in an important respect malleable. Far from being mere disembodied energy flow, the moving strings of words are engaged with by the viewer as part of the larger activity of becoming acquainted with, and moving around within the space of the gallery here and now. In her analysis of cyberspace as a realm into which the user can so very easily be seduced, N. Katherine Hayles maintains the idea established in the fiction of William Gibson that what connects with a computer's data banks is the 'human sensorium'; which is to say that it is the brain and nervous system that becomes linked into the computer's circuitry.[8] The body, somehow, and however notionally, gets left behind. Michel Serres appears to reiterate this view in his questioning of what it means to think of a 'here and now' in relation to a flow:

> *Maintenant*, now. What is the *maintenant*? The present
> participle of a verb like hold (*tenir*) in the hand (*main*), or
> to maintain. Maintenance. Now this solid object, the stature

of a god, tablet or basin, I hold or have it in hand. I cannot do this for a liquid, or fluid in general. Now time flows. I no more have time in hand than I can dam the water with my palm. Montaigne plunged his into the water: if he does not move it the current flows by running through his fingers and around his palm; if he withdraws it, he does not keep a drop. There is no *main-tenant*, no maintenance, *quod erat demonstrandum.*[9]

But then we think of Goethe, who speaks in his poem 'Lied und Gebilde', of what exquisite pleasure it is to plunge our fingers into the Euphrates and to let them drift to and fro in the liquid element. 'And when the poet's pure hand scoops water,' concludes Goethe, 'the water will become form.'[10] More recently, of course, Robert Smithson addressed the complex of connections between language and material, between the mental and the physical, between time flow and spatial disposition, and between the specifics of geographical location and placement in the generic space of a gallery:

> One's mind and the earth are in a constant state of erosion,
> mental rivers wear away abstract banks, brain waves
> undermine cliffs of thought, ideas decompose into stones
> of unknowing, and conceptual crystallisations break apart
> into deposits of gritty reason. Vast moving faculties occur in
> this geological miasma, and they move in the most physical
> way. This movement seems motionless, yet it crushes
> the landscape of logic under glacial reveries. This slow
> flowage makes one conscious of the turbidity of thinking.
> Slump, debris slides, avalanches all take place within the
> cracking limits of the brain. The entire body is pulled into
> the cerebral sediment, where particles and fragments make
> themselves known as solid consciousness. A bleached and
> fractured world surrounds the artist. To organise this mess
> of corrosion into patterns, grids, and subdivisions is an
> aesthetic process that has scarcely been touched.[11]

Thomson and Craighead's art touches this aesthetic process; they clearly see that the new technology with which they predominantly work, and whose specific attributes they analyse and exploit, is in many respects but an extension of the industrial legacy that preoccupied artists such as Smithson. 'Of course traditionally the railway, cars, and air-travel become very much about infrastructural growth,' says Thomson, 'and historically they are about colonisation — certainly with the railway. So we've found ourselves looking at these old networking technologies in this new networked world.'[12] And just as, too, Smithson placed the anonymous, general gallery space and the multifarious, inchoate world in relationship through his articulation of the site/non-site duality, Thomson and Craighead make it abundantly evident to us that the tension between the active and passive aspects of our involvement in their works, and the contrast between the physical dimensions of a room and the abstract expanses of cyberspace, are both specific and productive. They make a point, for example, of always citing the URL for any material they appropriate. This is an act of common courtesy, of course, but its significance lies more in the stress it places on the fact that the resource is unique, and that it is locatable. That we cannot immediately identify the particular server on which the file sits is immaterial; its locatability can be simply demonstrated by our typing an address and hitting return. In locating it we help to locate ourselves in our own, shared environment. We find this writ large in *Weather Gauge*. A wall of display screens gives information on time and temperature. The temperatures, given in both Fahrenheit and Celsius, differ from screen to screen, and the times do too, so we can infer that they relate either to different global locations at a single instant, or to a certain place at various times. Every few minutes the screens are wiped and get updated with new information, at which time we can see that each carries information from a different city around the world. The time is now, always now, and the information on the screens is telling us what the world is like, here and there, in this now.

1   Michel Foucault, 'What is an Author', in J. V. Harari (ed), *Textual Strategies: Perspectives in Post-Structuralist Criticism*, Cornell University Press, Ithaca, NY, 1979, p160

2   Timothy Allen Jackson, 'Towards a New Media Aesthetic', in D. Trend (ed), *Reading Digital Culture*, Blackwell, Oxford, p351. Paul Virilio develops his ideas on picnolepsis in *The Aesthetics of Disappearance*, Semiotext(e),

Brooklyn, NY, 1991

3   See, for example, Peter Dallow, 'The Space of Information: Digital Media
    as Simulation of the Analogical Mind', in S. R. Munt (ed), *Technospaces:
    Inside the New Media*, Continuum, 2001, pp57-70

4   William J. Mitchell, *Me ++: The Cyborg Self and the Networked City*, MIT,
    Cambridge, Mass, 2003, pp135-137

5   Alison Craighead in an interview with Charlotte L Frost, for
    www.rhizome.org, June 2003

6   Jon Thomson in an interview with Kris Cohen, 'The Wrong Categories' in
    Tom Corby (ed): *Network Art: Practices and Positions*, Taylor and Francis,
    2005

7   David Sanford Horner, 'Cyborgs and Cyberspace: Personal Identity and
    Moral Agency', in Munt, op cit, p83

8   N. Katherine Hayles, 'The Seductions of Cyberspace', in Trend, op cit,
    p306

9   Michel Serres, *The Birth of Physics*, Clinamen Press, Manchester, 2000,
    p152

10 J. W. von Goethe, *Selected Verse*, edited by D. Luke, Penguin,
    Harmondsworth, 1964, p236: *Schöpft des Dichters reine Hand/Wasser
    wird sich ballen.*

11 Robert Smithson, 'A Sedimentation of the Mind: Earth Projects', in *El
    Paisaje Entrópico*, IVAM, Valencia, 1993, p286

12 Jon Thomson in an interview with Kris Cohen, op cit

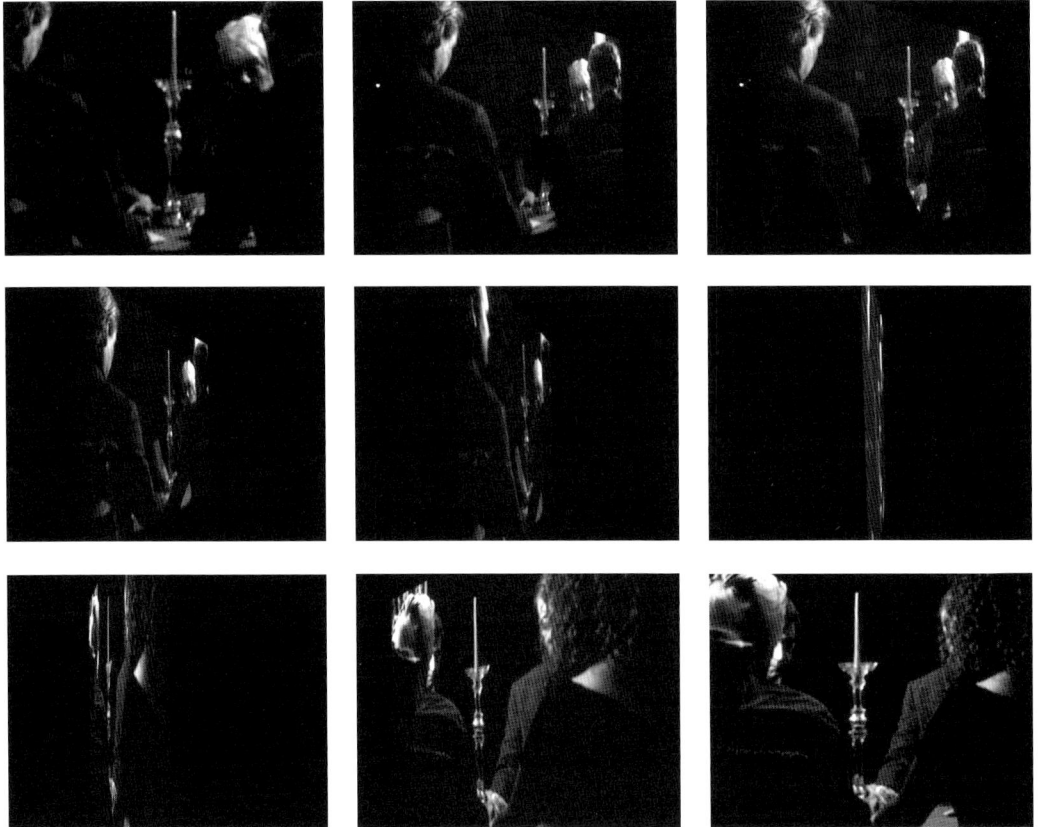

obituary

A seance shot from two opposite angles is represented on both sides of a suspended screen, allowing visitors to circle the table depicted in the seance as they walk around the screen, switching from one side to the other. The medium's face is blocked out in the manner often used in television to preserve anonymity. A voice reads a melange of found birthday card greetings and epitaphs, which become more layered as the seance reaches its climax.

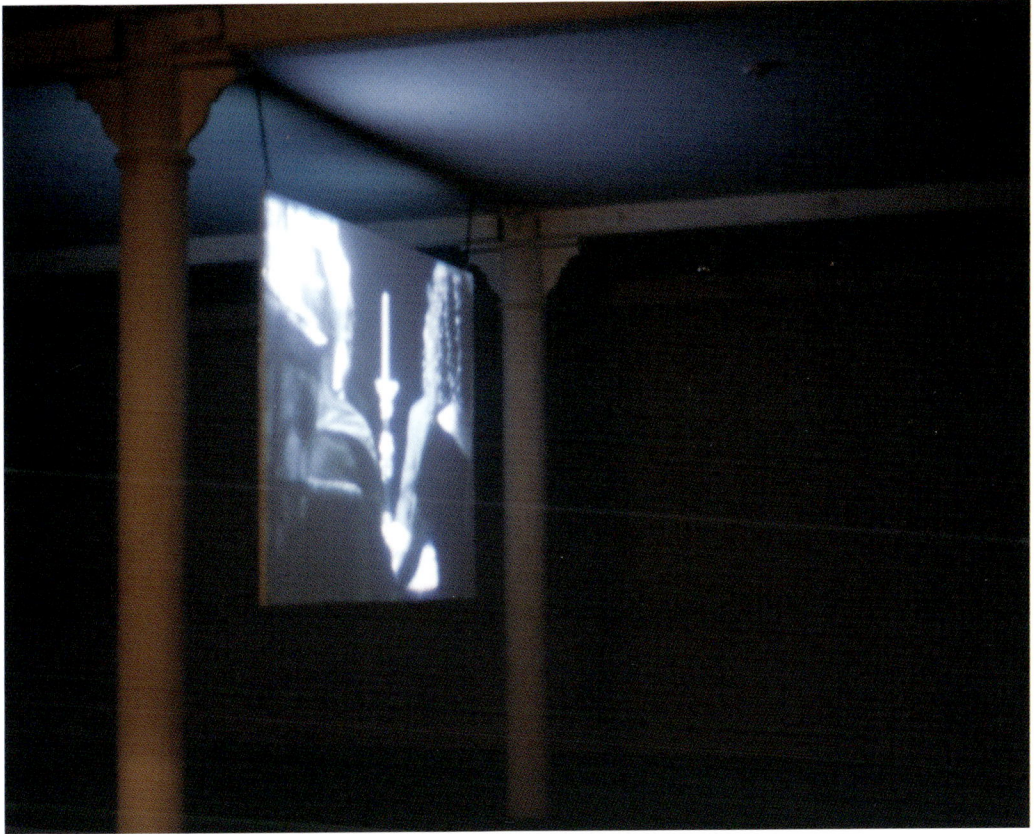

pet pages
http://www.pet-pages.org

'Pet Pages' is a gateway to a whole host of pre-existing websites about other people's pets. A kind of online documentary that charted this phenomenon at a time when how the web might be used was still very much up for grabs. On visiting the 'Pet Pages' website, your desktop is littered with windows that resemble a deck of cards — each card providing a link to a respective pet home page.

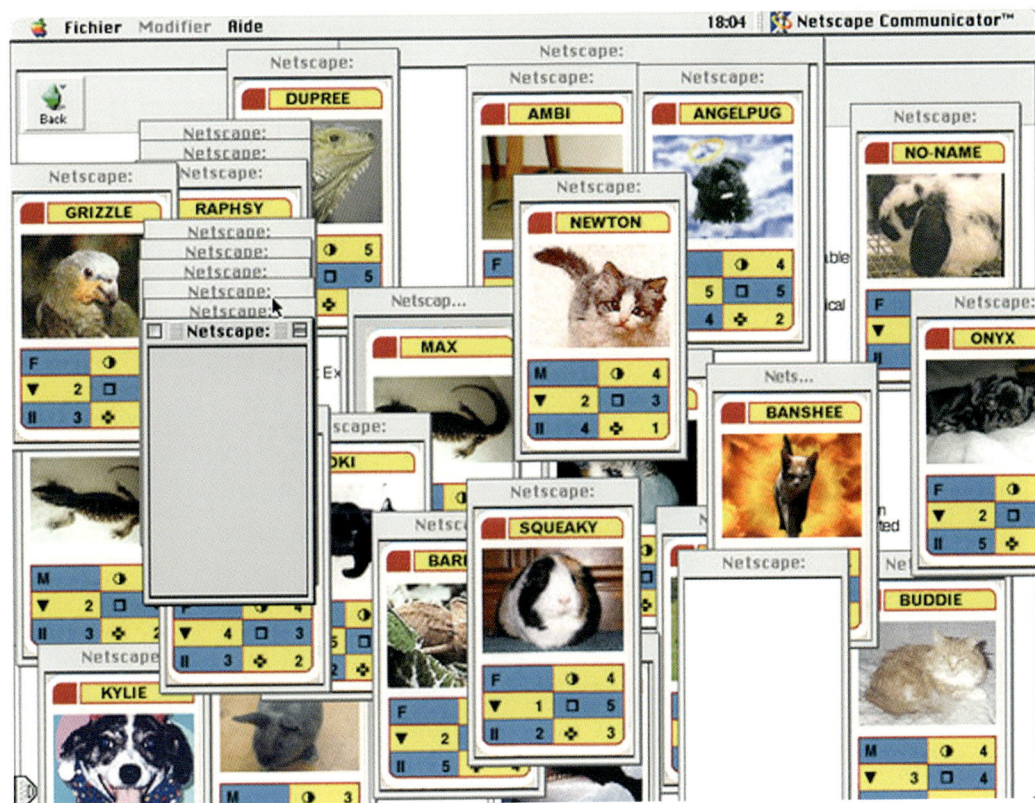

19

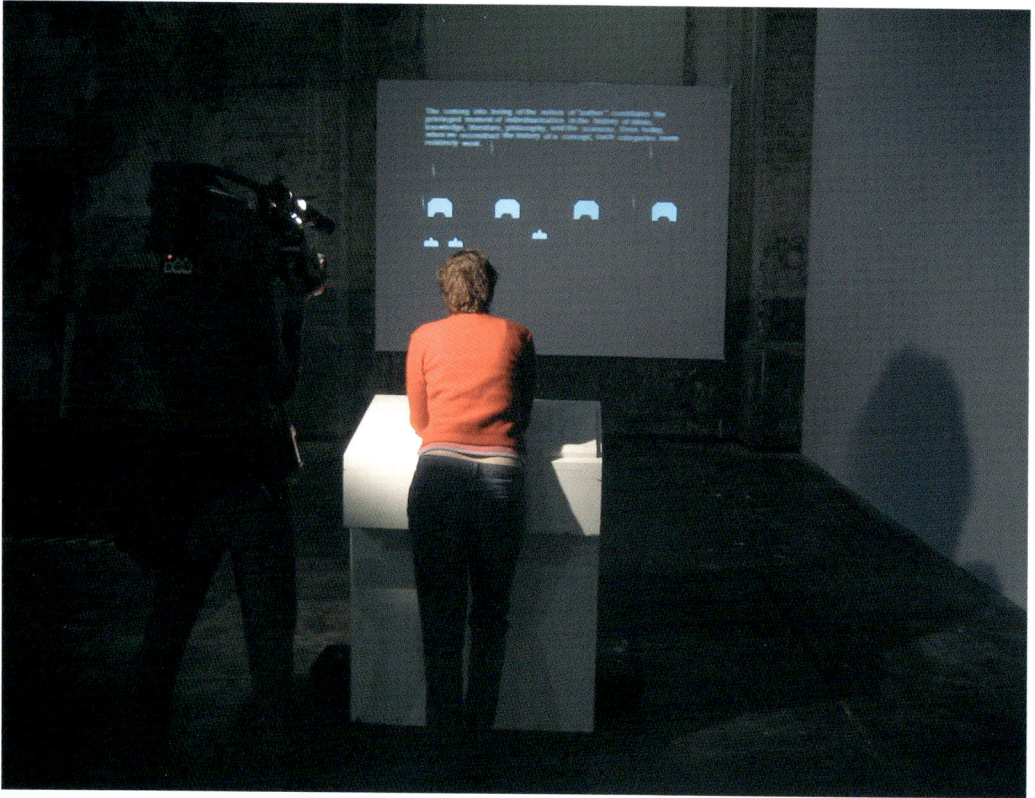

triggerhappy
http://www.triggerhappy.org

'Triggerhappy' is a simple re-working of the classic arcade game, 'Space Invaders'. Rather than defending against wave after wave of pixellated aliens, players must shoot up a series of text extracts taken from Michel Foucault's essay, 'What is an Author?' The game has nine levels, each with their own soundtrack taken from anonymous shortwave radio broadcasts sometimes referred to as Numbers Stations.

The coming into being of the notion of "author" constitutes the privileged moment of individualisation in the history of ideas, knowledge, literature,   and the sciences. Even today, when we   of a concept, such categories seem relatively weak.

Writing is an interplay of signs arranged less according to its signified content than according to the very nature of the signifier. Writing unfolds   game (jeu) that invariably goes beyond its own rules and   limits.

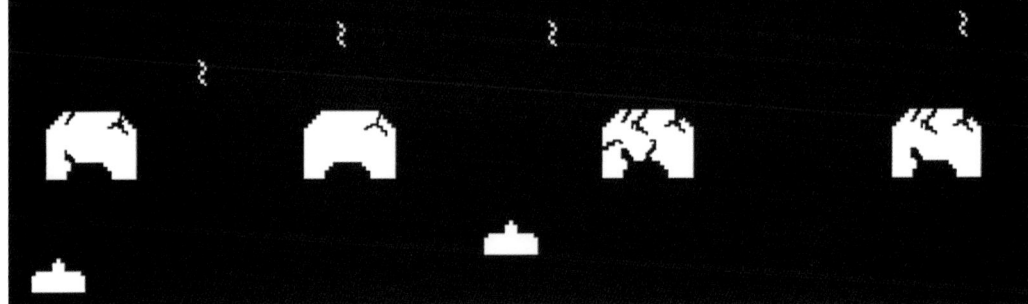

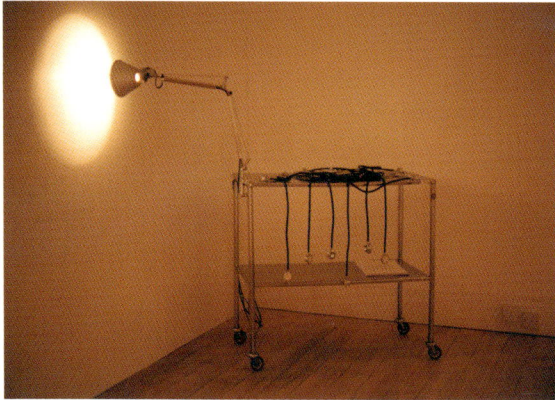

speaking in tongues

In 'Speaking in Tongues', gallery visitors are encouraged to use a stethoscope to listen to a wall behind which banks of speakers endlessly play back audible fragments plucked from the ether — mobile phone calls, broadcast radio transmissions, taxi radio etc. Meanwhile, a projection of animated mouse arrows perpetually pointing and clicking plays on the opposite wall.

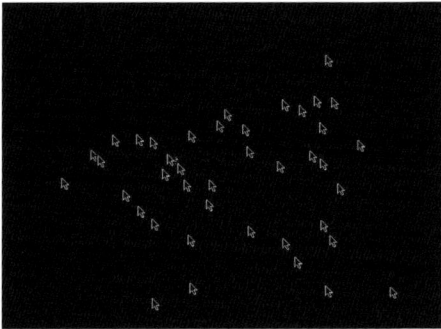
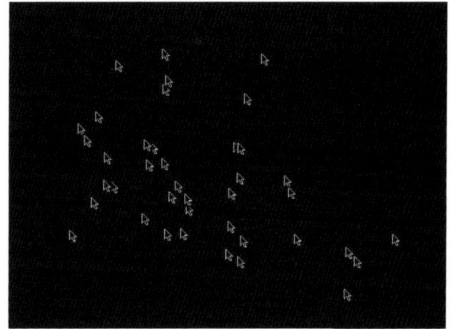
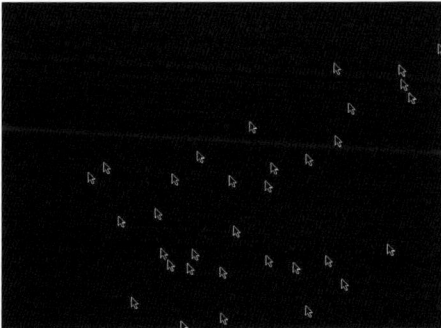
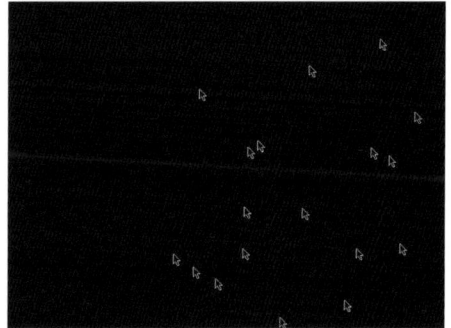
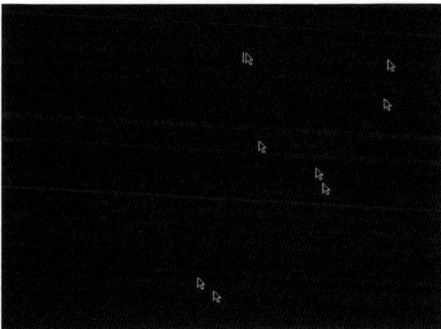

"Yeah."

"Do you think I should leave this cell-phone on and you ring me just before I… [LAUGHS]"

"All these people were laughing cos I kind of jumped… [UNCLEAR] …said Thameslink

"Yes all right."

"It's just amazing that erm…"

"Mm."

"But I, but when I just got the phone now, it seemed to be on, and I hadn't turned it on"

"Oh well."

"It had that cell-net thing on it."

"Well it must be on then. Well leave it on, and I'll give you a ring later on."

[LAUGHS]

"Ok."

"Do you think that's funny?

"Yes I do."

"Ok darling. I have this terror of falling asleep."

"Yes, Yes."

"Because I never expected to fall asleep on that short journey."

"No course not."

"But Leslie had a nice time, and I had a wonderful time with the children."

"Good, good."

"Right."

"But that brochure if you open it up doesn't seem to have anything about erm, Belle Isle. It is the right one, she got hers and…"

"Oh I see."

"But look and see if you can find it. I couldn't find anything about Belle Isle."

"Oh OK."

"Right Darling Bye."

"Right Bye-bye."

[SIGNAL ENDS]

"Why do you love me?"
"Cos I do."
"Why do you want to be with me? Why did you buy them shoes today? 'Because I did' —that's not an answer!"
[UNCLEAR]
"[SIGH] Can we ever right?"
"Hmm."
"Have a time, yeah?"
"Mm."
"When we are together, right, and share our emotions and passion?"
[UNCLEAR]
"And I'm not talking about just one-off, right? As in wasn't it nice, I mean all the time."
[UNCLEAR]
"Well put some time to one side in the evenings, where we're together, where we just sit together, and talk together, and are together and be together. Can we do that?"
[SILENCE]
"No we can't."
"What's the point in asking then?"
"Because you can't do it, all right? Do you want me to answer it for ya?"
"No I don't. I'm putting the phone down now."
"Oh, if you put the phone down on me I'm goi-"

[SIGNAL ENDS]

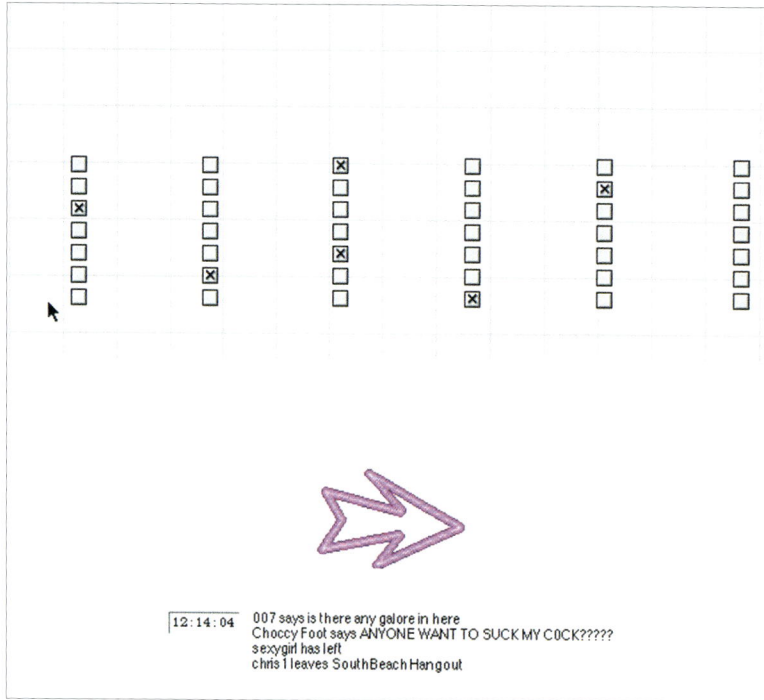

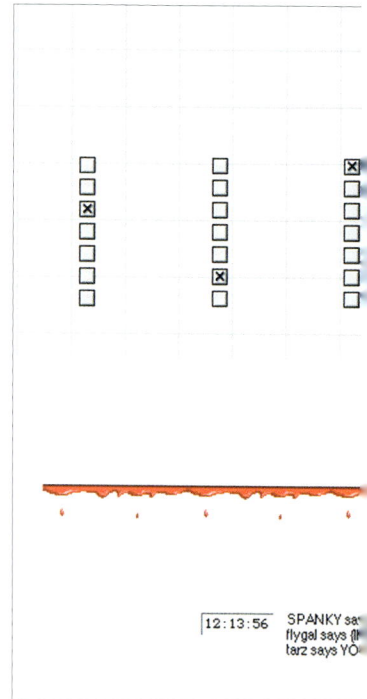

| 12:14:04 | 007 says is there any galore in here
Choccy Foot says ANYONE WANT TO SUCK MY C0CK?????
sexygirl has left
chris 1 leaves South Beach Hangout |

| 12:13:56 | SPANKY sa'
flygal says {l
tarz says YO |

weightless

http://www.thomson-craighead.net/w/

A website where visitors are able to navigate a database of animated web graphics, chat room transcripts and music MIDI files in a manner that in part references a television format. The anodyne music files resemble a soundtrack while the animated graphics and chat room logs act as picture and subtitling. As all this material was gathered and found online in 1998, the work also acts as a social document of early web usage.

DRE DOG!!!

NCH OF PU$$Y LICKERS

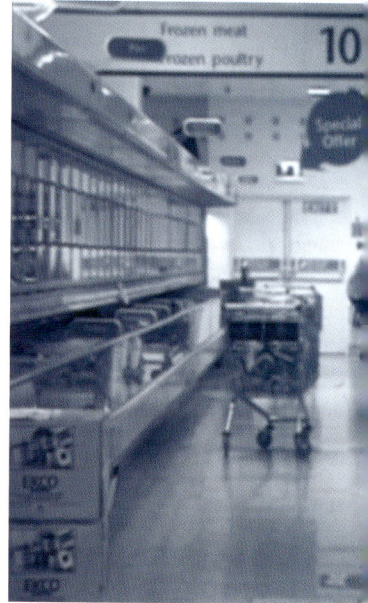

shopping

'Shopping' is based on a supermarket trolley dash organised by 'Take a Break' magazine during October 1999. The competition, which took place in a supermarket on the edge of London, was documented on video and focused on the action taking place in three adjacent aisles. It is these three recordings that form the basis of the installation where the trolley dash is replayed endlessly in the gallery as a monumental video triptych.

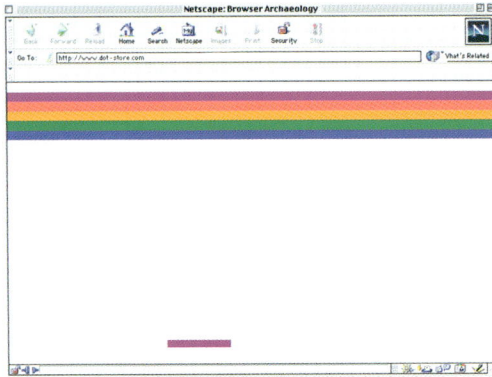

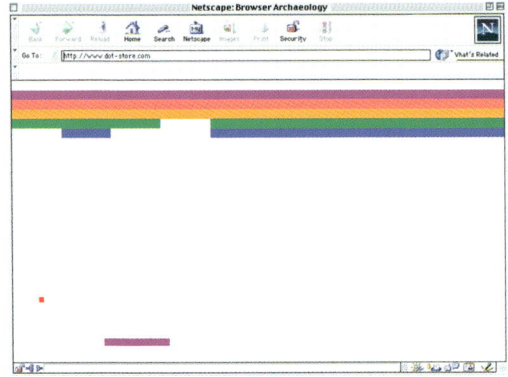

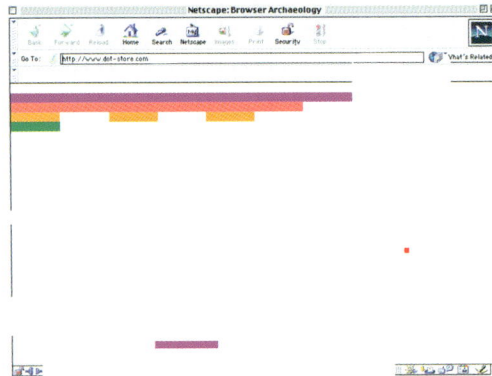

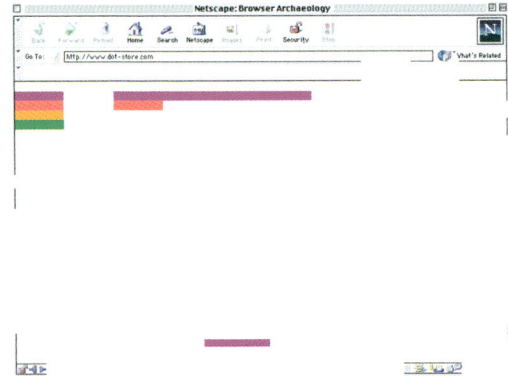

browser archaeology

http://www.dot-store.com

**'Browser Archaeology' is a playable online re-creation of Atari's arcade classic video game 'Breakout'.
In this version however, the game play extends beyond the rows of colourful bricks and starts taking the
browser apart as well.**

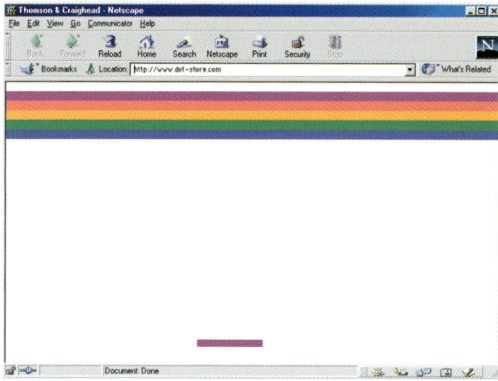

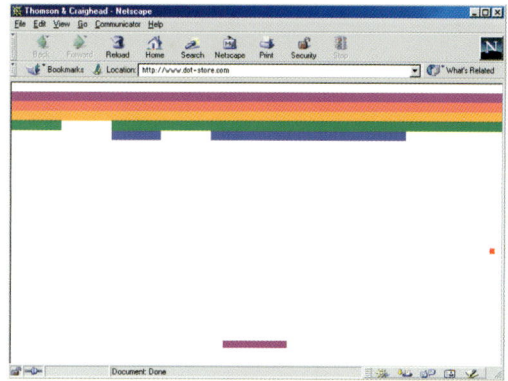

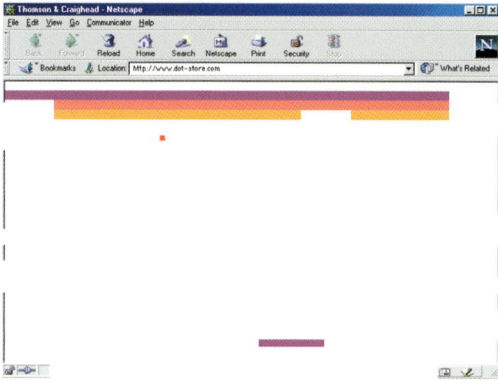

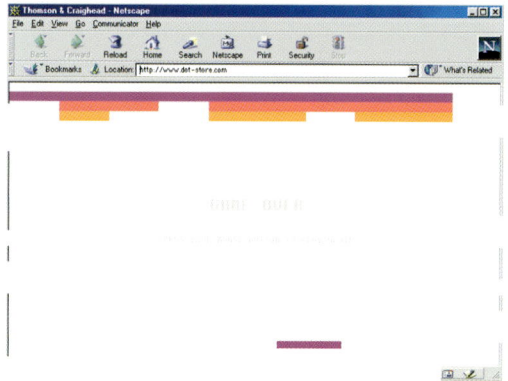

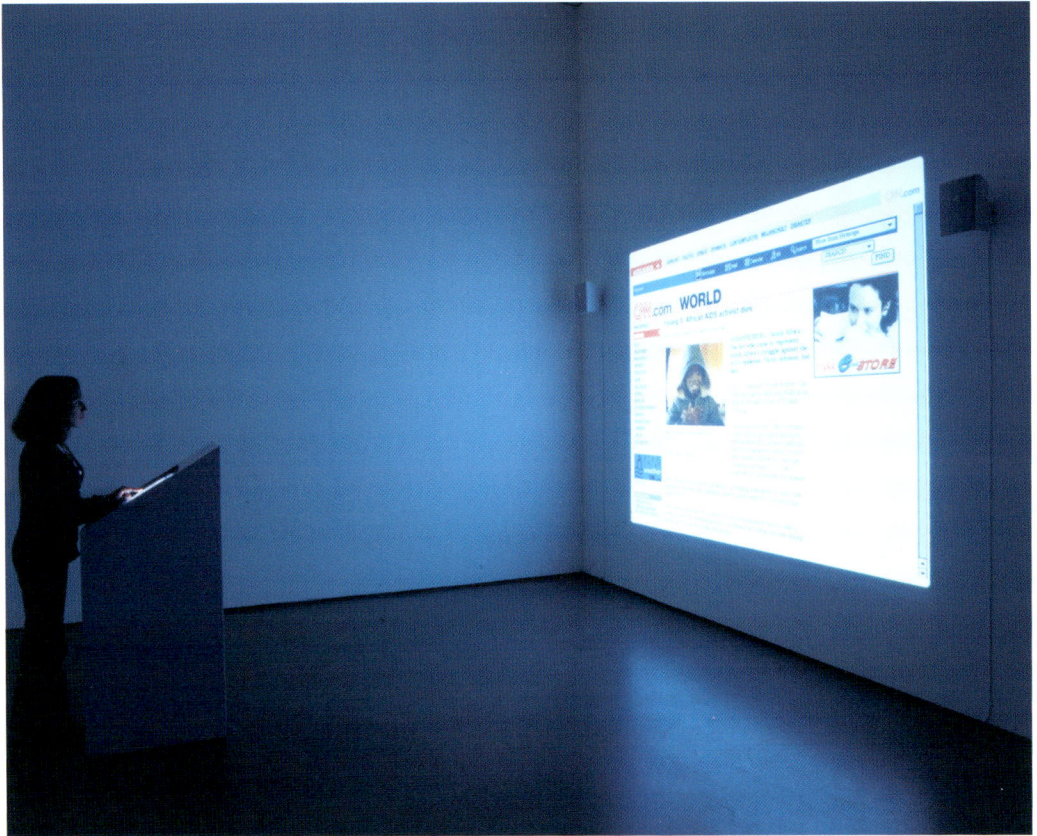

cnn interactive just got more interactive
http://www.cnnextra.net

'CNN Interactive just got more interactive' exists as both a website and a gallery installation where visitors can add a variety of emotively titled soundtracks to the monolithic CNN Interactive website in an attempt to further mediate a moment of infotainment — bringing a cinematic conceit to this ever changing global newsfeed.

trooper

'Trooper' is a short video, where a news report taken from a CNN webcast is both repeated and sped up systematically. In doing so, the authority of the seemingly factual and neutral newscast is eroded, deconstructed and ultimately exposed as a fictive conceit.

01.01.01. e-poltergeist.
Banner ad cycle.

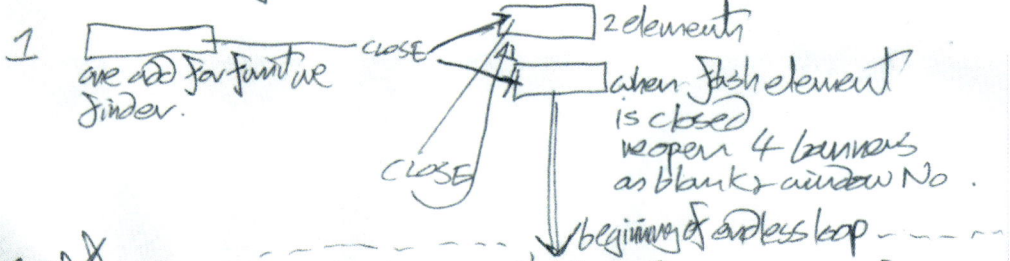

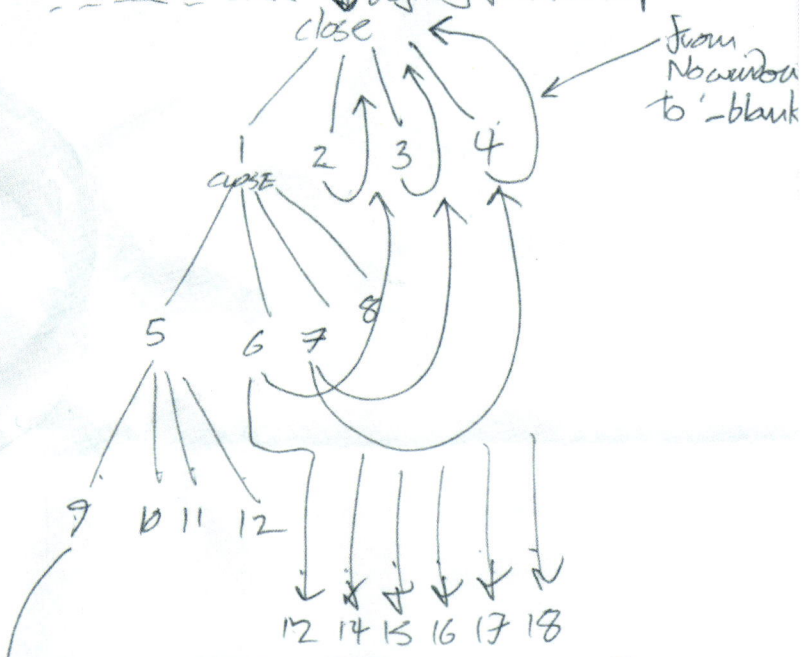

1   [box] are ad for furniture finder.   CLOSE → [box] 2 elements

when flash element is closed reopen 4 banners as blank window No.

CLOSE

- - - - - beginning of endless loop - - - - - - -

close ←   from No window to '_blank

close   1   2   3   4
CLOSE

5   6   7   8

9   10 11 12

12 14 15 16 17 18

TOWARDS OPEN [blank]
no. of window will vary depending on how often banners are closed.

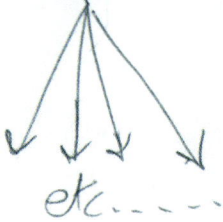

etc.......

Some windows rearrange
Some proliferate.
The more end users closes them the more will open ideally.
until either: BROWSER CRASHES.

36

e-poltergeist

Archived at http://www.thomson-craighead.net

'e-poltergeist' was designed to be encountered unwittingly by web users, where a perpetual and virtually unstoppable cycle of search engine results, banner ads and moving windows interrupts normal use of our browser. Such relative chaos carries a series of messages from the live search engine data — messages that seem to be addressing the end user: 'Is anyone there?', 'Can anyone hear me?', 'Please help me!', 'Nobody cares!'

telephony

'Telephony' lets gallery visitors dial into a wall-based grid of 42 mobile phones, which in turn begin to call each other and create a piece of music. Each phone has been individually programmed with a different ringtone, which, played en masse, create various harmonic layers all of which are based in some way on the popular and prevalent NokiaTune. The more people who dial into the work (whether inside or beyond the gallery walls) the more complex and layered the audio becomes.

```
Date: 25/01/02
Subject's name:  Rotterdamse Sprekende Klok
------------------------------------------------------------
Truster System - Profile Report
------------------------------------------------------------


> "Excited" samples : (66%)
> "Stressed" samples : (33%)
> "Uncertain" samples : (8%)
> "Voice manipulation" samples : (0%)
> "Outsmarting" samples : (0%)


------------------------------------------------------------

> "Intensive Thinking" samples : (79%)


------------------------------------------------------------

> "Inaccuracy" samples : (4%)
> "False Statement" samples : (20%)


------------------------------------------------------------

>> Suggested Analysis

The subject was highly excited during the conversation

The subject was stressed in some parts of the conversation.

The subject was not confident in all his words.

------------------------------------------------------------

Thank you for using Truster - Your Personal Truth Verifier
```

```
Date: 25/01/02
Subject's name:  The Speaking Clock, UK-British Telecom
-----------------------------------------------------------
Truster System - Profile Report
-----------------------------------------------------------


> "Excited" samples : (0%)
> "Stressed" samples : (41%)
> "Uncertain" samples : (7%)
> "Voice manipulation" samples : (0%)
> "Outsmarting" samples : (0%)


-----------------------------------------------------------


> "Intensive Thinking" samples : (7%)


-----------------------------------------------------------


> "Inaccuracy" samples : (7%)
> "False Statement" samples : (3%)


-----------------------------------------------------------


>> Suggested Analysis

The subject was not excited AT ALL during the conversation.

The subject was stressed in some parts of the conversation.

The subject was not confident in all his words.

-----------------------------------------------------------

The subject might exaggerate from time to time.

-----------------------------------------------------------

Thank you for using Truster - Your Personal Truth Verifier
```

driving through las vegas

In 'Driving Through Las Vegas' gallery visitors are able to variously soundtrack a movie depicting a high-speed drive along the Las Vegas main strip by plugging headphones into a grid of 32 jack sockets each feeding its own internet radio feed in to the gallery.

```
01 Bobby Rock
02 Asian Vibrations
03 SF Bay Area Smooth Jazz
04 Cinemascape Radio
05 Prema Yoga Radio Meditation
06 Acid Radio
07 Amharic Music Radio Ethiopia
08 Country Golden Jukebox
09 Planet Tonga
10 The 1960's Chart Boy
11 Radio Xiaos: Hindi Bollywood
12 Bible Verses of Hope with Piano Music
13 M I C R O D O T S
14 Persian Musik Radio
15 Yesterday's Gardenias
16 Netgoths - Gothic Radio
17 The Sound Of Love: 35 years of love songs
18 Alaska's Tundra Trash
19 The Holy Quran & Islamic Songs
20 Moon Base Alpha
21 Modern Flamenco Guitars
22 SoundCraze - Today's music from  today's artists
23 Ballroom Tunes
24 Big Up The London Massive
25 Russian Film, TV and Cartoon Song Classics
26 Chinese Oldies
27 Mostly Australian Music
28 Anime Hardcore Radio
29 Great choral music
30 Rastafari Music
31 Krishna chanting with cool pop
32 Poizen Ivy's Las Vegas Tiki Lounge
```

dot-store

http://www.dot-store.com

'dot-store' used an e-shop environment as a context within which a series of artworks could be delivered both on- and offline. From October 2002 until January 2005, 'dot-store' produced and sold a range of low cost multiples that referenced both the history of the world wide web and the popular explosion of mobile communications towards the turn of the millennium. Products included sealed walkmans containing scanned mobile phone conversations, temporary tattoos, mobile ringtones and logos, downloadable games and tea towels sporting Google search engine results for queries like, 'Please help me', 'Please listen to me' or 'Is anybody there?'

http://www.dot-store.com/

Google

dot-store

Product Finder

VIEW BASKET | HELP | MAILING LIST

WELCOME TO DOT-STORE

A World Wide Web of vintage products and services...

A limited edition of thirty specially prepared personal stereos, playing scanned materia from early 1990's!.

UK £29.99

Cursor animation lenticular badges. Mac OS & Windows designs. Exclusive only to dot-store.com. Packs of two.

UK £1.99

Google search-engine result tea towels, each. 4designs. 100% pure Egyptian Cotton and machine washable.

UK £7.99

MESS M S code: 4503
HELL code: 4505
snotbboy code: 4506

Ringtones & logos brought to you in association with www.artones.net for less than many other providers!

UK £2.50

Find out how much time remains until dot-store goes for auction on ebay by clicking here

---

http://www.dot-store.com/

Google

dot-store

Tea-towels (BEST SELLER!)

VIEW BASKET | HELP | MAILING LIST

TEATOWELS OF THE WEB

Please help me   Can you hear me?   Please listen to me   Is anybody there?

For more information, simply click on one of the four towel designs.

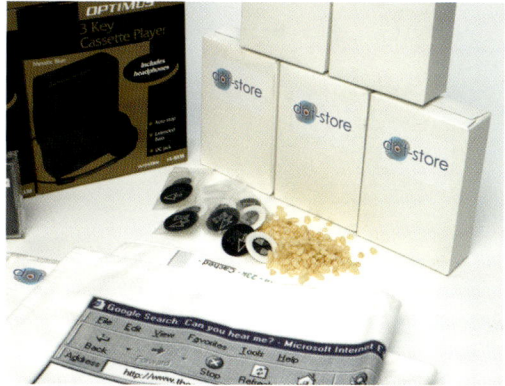

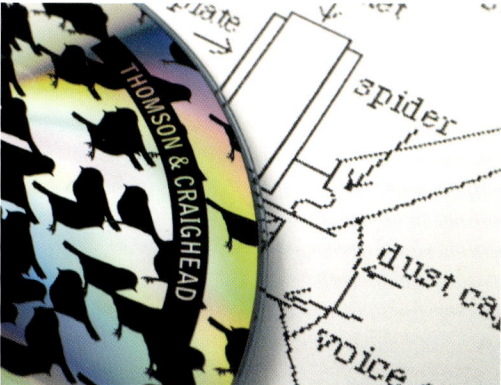

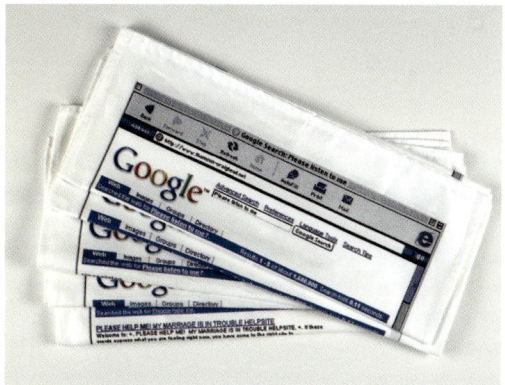

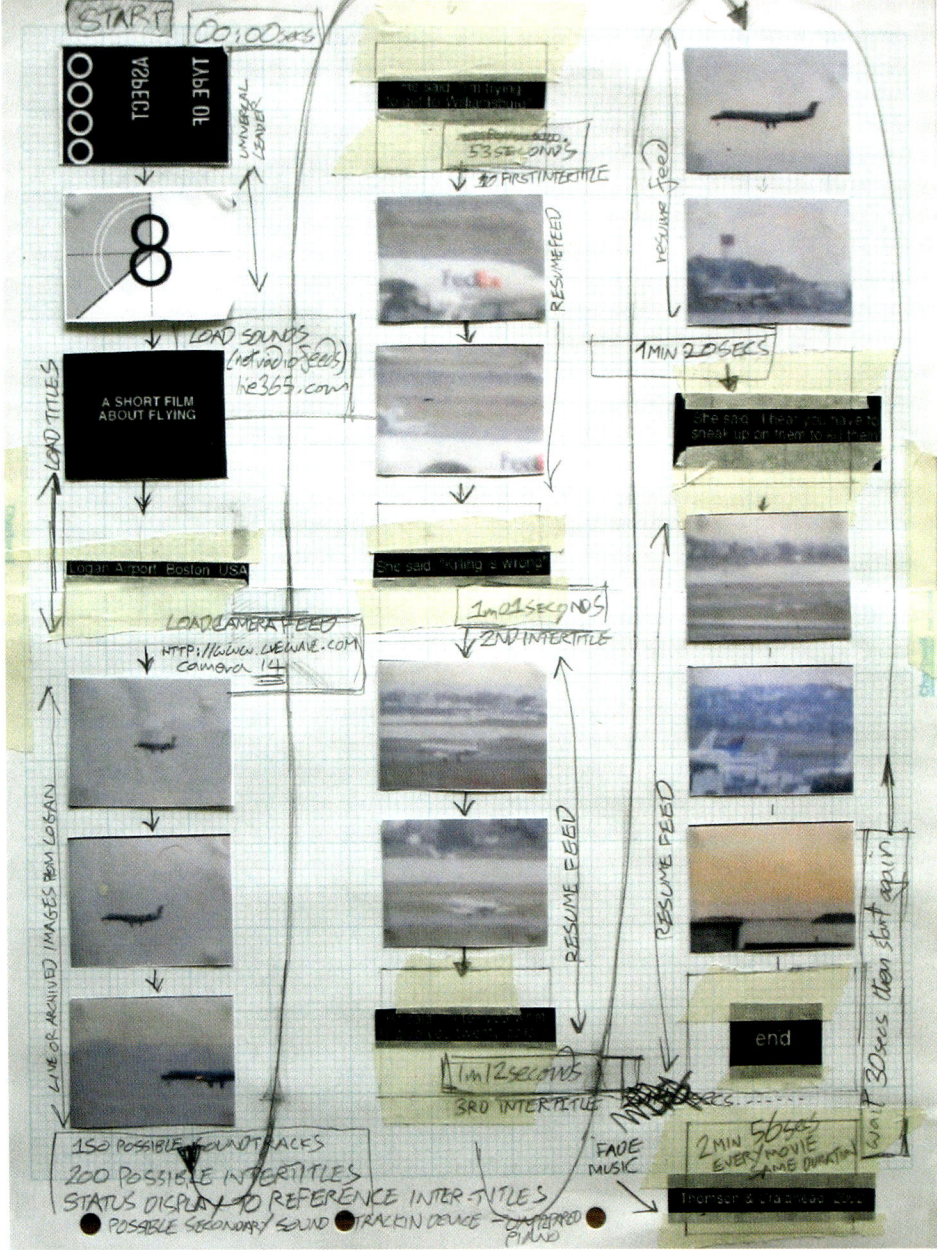

SHORT FILMS ABOUT FLYING
TEMPLATE • STORY BOARD

START
00:00secs

SPECT
TYPE 01

UNIVERSAL LEADER

LOAD TITLES

8

LOAD SOUNDS
(not radio secs)
lie365.com

A SHORT FILM
ABOUT FLYING

Logan Airport Boston USA

LOAD CAMERA FEED
HTTP://www.liveWAVE.com
camera 14

LIVE OR ARCHIVED IMAGES FROM LOGAN

She said "flying is wrong"

1m01seconds
2ND INTERTITLE

RESUME FEED

1m12seconds
3RD INTERTITLE

FADE
MUSIC

150 POSSIBLE SOUNDTRACKS
200 POSSIBLE INTERTITLES
STATUS DISPLAY TO REFERENCE INTER-TITLES
POSSIBLE SECONDARY SOUND TRACK IN DEVICE

She said "I'm flying
I could be Johannesburg"

53 SECONDS
FIRST INTERTITLE

FedEx

RESUME FEED

resume feed

1MIN 20SECS

She said "I hear you have to
sneak up on them to kill them"

RESUME FEED

RESUME FEED

end

wait 30secs then start again

2MIN 56secs
EVERY MOVIE
SAME DURATION

Thomson & Craighead 2002

SCATTERED PIANO

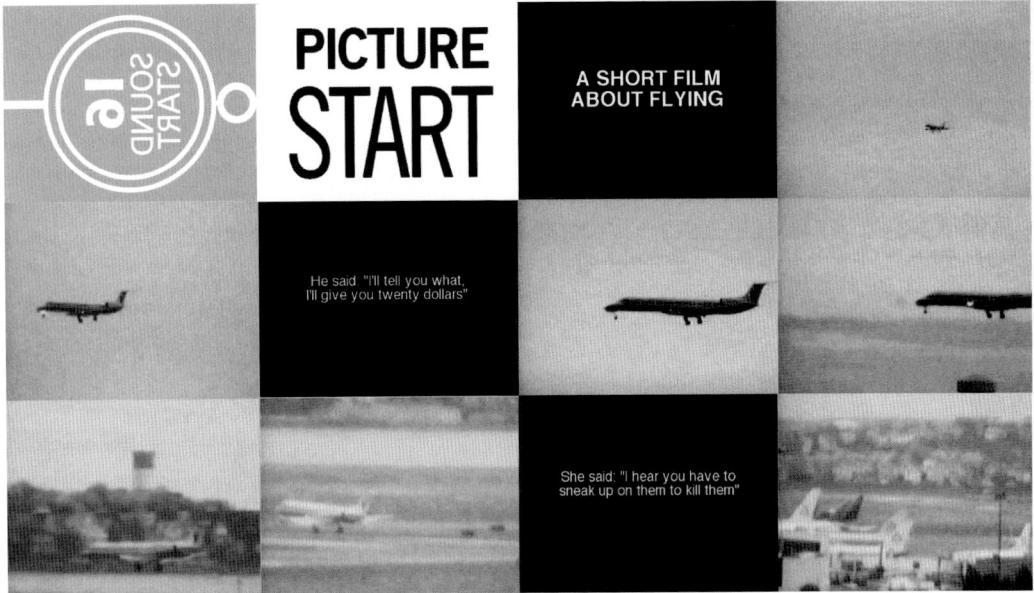

PICTURE
START

16 SOUND START

A SHORT FILM
ABOUT FLYING

He said "I'll tell you what,
I'll give you twenty dollars"

She said: "I hear you have to
sneak up on them to kill them"

short films about flying

'Short Films about Flying' is an automatic machine that generates an endless open edition of unique cinematic works in real time from a live camera feed from Boston's Logan Airport, randomly grabbed web radio feeds and a database of texts taken from websites, chat rooms, message boards etc.

A SHORT FILM ABOUT FLYING

He said: "Help me, don't let me die"

She said: "I just scream into the mic and tell them to stop calling"

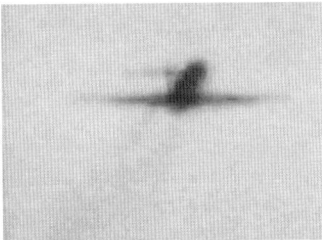

He said that the match no longer mattered

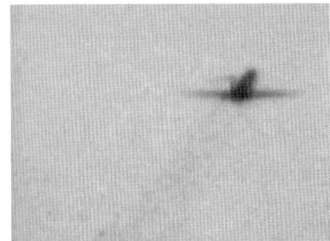

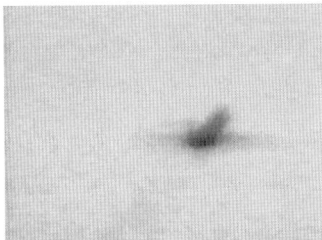

She said she'd love me forever

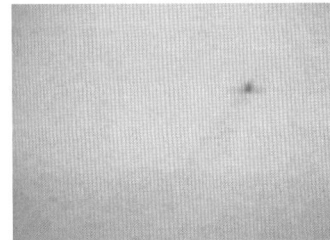

51

decorative newsfeeds

'Decorative Newsfeeds' presents up-to-the-minute headline news from around the world as a series of eye-catching animations, allowing gallery visitors to keep informed while contemplating a kind of ready-made sculpture or automatic drawing.

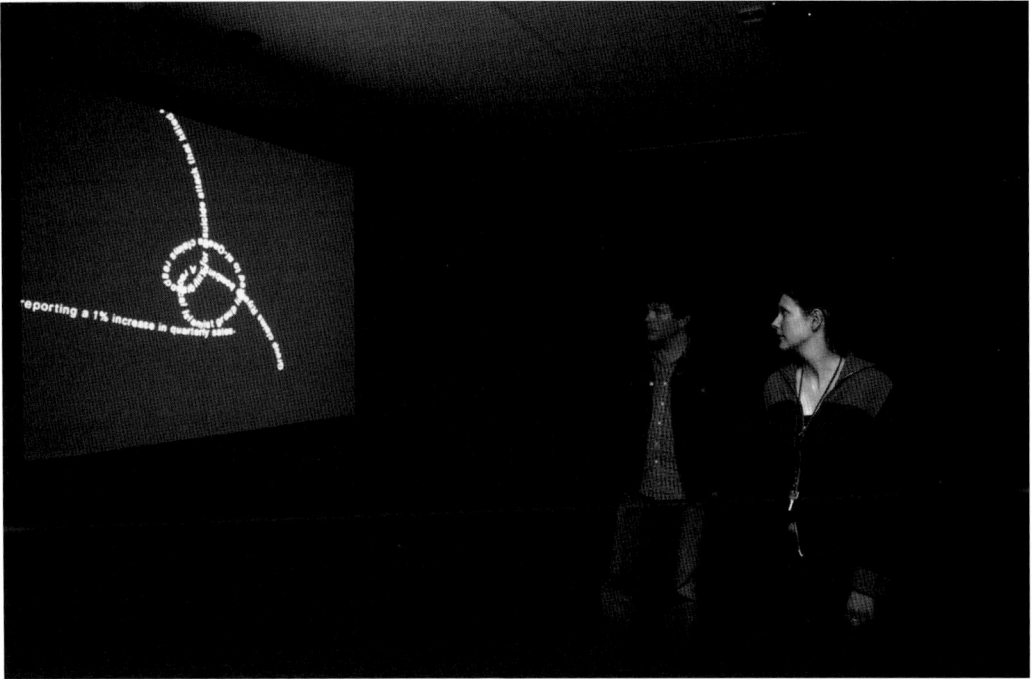

Panel 1
says it will cut 3,280 jobs today

reports a sharp rise in profits.

Rosneft denies China Yugansk Germany and link: Confusion about the role of Ch...

Rosneft

Panel 2
a sharp rise in profits.

Rosneft denies China Yugansk link

Yugansk

in the sale of Russia's

Confusion about the role of Chinese ...gas deepened on Wednesd...

Panel 3
in the sale of Russia's Yuganskneftegas deepened on Wednesday.

Mandela makes poverty plea: Nelson Mandela urges world leaders not to "...

Panel 4
Reid blames 'socialist...' fallen in London

Reid blames 'socialist disarmament'; Blaming the IRA for a £26m ra...

...ders not to "look the other way" on world poverty s...

Panel 5
Tsunami baby under police guard: Sri Lanka's tsunami 'miracle...

...as been reported.

former Home Secretary David Blunkett has given birth to a son. If...

Panel 6
diplomatic dispute between the Col...

...nations.

The Colombian and Venezuelan leaders are ...meet to try to resolve a di...

Incapacity Benefit to be...

Venezuela ...try to Colombia to end row.

MP faces Commons suspension: Tory MP Jonathan

tsunami victims leaves, as emergency operations are scaled down.

template cinema

http://www.templatecinema.com

A website where visitors can watch a selection of lo-fi movies made from existing data flow accessed in real time from the web. As the live web-cams and sound files that make up each movie are accessed rather than appropriated, each work of template cinema is simply a list of instructions — not unlike the drawings of Sol Lewitt for example. Unlike Lewitt's drawings, these instructions actually execute themselves.

Template_Cinema

http://www.templatecinema.com

Template Cinema

> Welcome to Template Cinema on-line:
  Low-tech movies made from existing data appropriated in realtime from the world wide web

> You can launch any movie you want to see by clicking on its title

TITLE:	DURATION:	STATUS:	BROWSER COMPATABILITY:
A short Film about Nothing	3m 40s	Seems OK	Firefox / Explorer / Netscape
Five Ghosts floating unawares	5m 34s	Broken	Firefox / Explorer / Netscape
A short Film set in New Mexico	3m 23s	No Image	Firefox / Explorer / Netscape
A short Film where the dead speak	3m 00s	Seems OK	Firefox / Explorer / Netscape
A short Film set in Philadelphia	6m 43s	Seems OK	Firefox / Explorer / Netscape / Safari
A brief look at Desire	COMING	SOON	Firefox / Explorer / Netscape / Safari

> In order to watch these movies, you will need a well configured browser with javascript enabled and all the usual plug-ins installed. You must also be on a decent broadband connection as all images and sounds are streamed live from all over the world. In some cases you may also have to switch off popup window blocking.

> Please check back from time to time as new titles are configured and please report any bugs to look@templatecinema.com

> Template Cinema is being developed by London based artists Thomson & Craighead. Template Cinema first started in 2002 with a gallery installation called, 'Short Films about Flying.' You can find out more by visiting http://www.thomson-craighead.net and http://www.dot-store.com

> Missing a media player? ● Windows Media Player ● Quicktime Player ● Real Player

A SHORT FILM IN WHICH NOTHING
ACTUALLY HAPPENS....

BEGIN

FENGTH

BOTT

UNIVERSAL
LOADER

m   m
7
35   35

3

**PICTURE
START**

END LEADER

A short film in which nothing happens

TITLE ONE

Sunday, December 19 9:25 AM

START MUSK HERE

FunCoastFunCam, Sun Dec 19 11:18:12 2004

FunCoastFunCam, Sun Dec 19 11:36:32 2004

FunCoastFunCam, Sun Dec 19 11:25:01 2004

FunCoastFunCam, Sun Dec 19 11:23:15 2004

FunCoastFunCam, Sun Dec 19 10:13:53 2004

FunCoastFunCam, Sun Dec 19 10:14:55 2004

FunCoastFunCam, Sun Dec 19 10:17:46 2004

POSSIBLE
additional
live audio
for this one

8

end

WILL PINGING
ATTS SERVER
GENERATE
VOICE
OVER?

020474

Camera:
Live from Sandusky's Bay View
of Cedar Point in Erie County, Ohio
http://funcam.funcoast.com/high_framerates.html

Phone recording taken
from the virtual step of President
Johnson's phone line made in 1966.
http://audio01.archive.org/2/items/lbj860203/

END MUSK HERE
(stop loop)

Music by Travis Noble
http://www.timenoise.com/say_rain.html

RESET

TEMPLATECINEMA.COM

unprepared piano

In 'Unprepared Piano', a grand piano is connected to a database of music MIDI files appropriated and compiled from all over the web. This library of found data is then 'performed' automatically by the piano in the gallery with the full authority one associates with a concert grand piano. However, because the piano does not know what notation is contained in any given MIDI file, or more particularly what instruments this notation was created for in its original context, this 'unprepared' piano ends up rendering drum parts, string sections, piano parts, marimbas etc in awkward configurations and combinations.

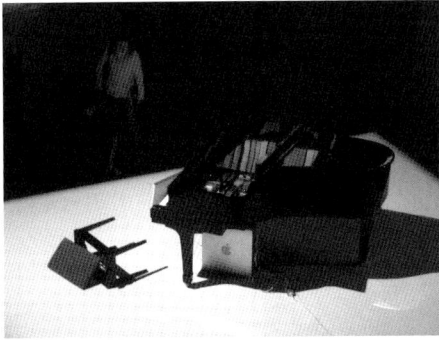

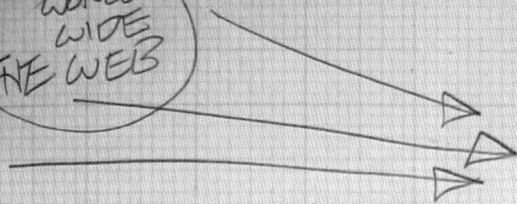

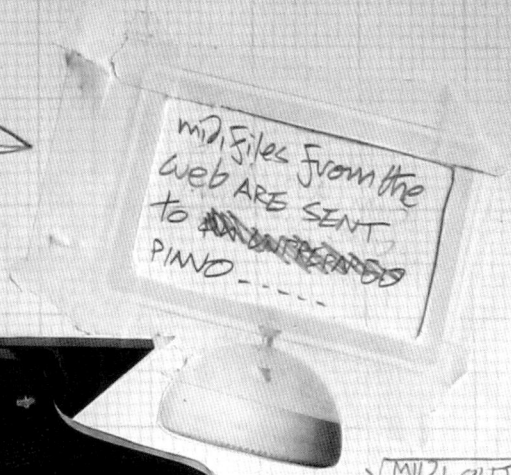

[ ] YOU HAVE REACHED AN AUTOMATED BEACON

erotic stories

CURRENT TIME = FRIDAY, JANUARY 14 12:23 PM
FIRST STARTED = 00.00HRS GMT ON 01ST JANUARY 2005

ID = TC001\LIVE_RELAY\DOGPILELIVESEARCHDATA0000F
ALWAYS VISIBLE AT: HTTP://WWW.AUTOMATEDBEACON.NET

CURRENTLY BROADCASTING ON THE FOLLOWING FREQUENCIES:
NONE

HTTP://WWW.THOMSON-CRAIGHEAD.NET

READ_ME

beacon
http://www.automatedbeacon.net

BEACON continuously relays live web searches as they are being made around the world, presenting them back in series and at regular intervals. Instigated to act as a silent witness, BEACON's feedback loop provides a global snapshot of ourselves to ourselves in real time.

[ ] YOU HAVE REACHED AN AUTOMATED BEACON

famous smoke

CURRENT TIME = FRIDAY, JANUARY 14 12:23 PM
FIRST STARTED = 00.00HRS GMT ON 01ST JANUARY 2005

ID = TC001\LIVE_RELAY\DOGPILELIVESEARCHDATA0000F
ALWAYS VISIBLE AT: HTTP://WWW.AUTOMATEDBEACON.NET

CURRENTLY BROADCASTING ON THE FOLLOWING FREQUENCIES:
NONE

HTTP://WWW.THOMSON-CRAIGHEAD.NET

READ_ME

[ ] YOU HAVE REACHED AN AUTOMATED BEACON

hsbc arena

CURRENT TIME = FRIDAY, JANUARY 14 12:23 PM
FIRST STARTED = 00.00HRS GMT ON 01ST JANUARY 2005

ID = TC001\LIVE_RELAY\DOGPILELIVESEARCHDATA0000F
ALWAYS VISIBLE AT: HTTP://WWW.AUTOMATEDBEACON.NET

CURRENTLY BROADCASTING ON THE FOLLOWING FREQUENCIES:
NONE

HTTP://WWW.THOMSON-CRAIGHEAD.NET

READ_ME

[ ] YOU HAVE REACHED AN AUTOMATED BEACON

marquee hire

CURRENT TIME = FRIDAY, JANUARY 14 12:24 PM
FIRST STARTED = 00.00HRS GMT ON 01ST JANUARY 2005

ID = TC001\LIVE_RELAY\DOGPILELIVESEARCHDATA0000F
ALWAYS VISIBLE AT: HTTP://WWW.AUTOMATEDBEACON.NET

CURRENTLY BROADCASTING ON THE FOLLOWING FREQUENCIES:
NONE

HTTP://WWW.THOMSON-CRAIGHEAD.NET

READ_ME

[ ] YOU HAVE REACHED AN AUTOMATED BEACON

"first blood" and photo

CURRENT TIME = FRIDAY, JANUARY 14 12:24 PM
FIRST STARTED = 00.00HRS GMT ON 01ST JANUARY 2005

ID = TC001\LIVE_RELAY\DOGPILELIVESEARCHDATA0000F
ALWAYS VISIBLE AT: HTTP://WWW.AUTOMATEDBEACON.NET

CURRENTLY BROADCASTING ON THE FOLLOWING FREQUENCIES:
NONE

HTTP://WWW.THOMSON-CRAIGHEAD.NET

READ_ME

[ ] YOU HAVE REACHED AN AUTOMATED BEACON

hp c2746b monitor

CURRENT TIME = FRIDAY, JANUARY 14 12:24 PM
FIRST STARTED = 00.00HRS GMT ON 01ST JANUARY 2005

ID = TC001\LIVE_RELAY\DOGPILELIVESEARCHDATA0000F
ALWAYS VISIBLE AT: HTTP://WWW.AUTOMATEDBEACON.NET

CURRENTLY BROADCASTING ON THE FOLLOWING FREQUENCIES:
NONE

HTTP://WWW.THOMSON-CRAIGHEAD.NET

READ_ME

[ ] YOU HAVE REACHED AN AUTOMATED BEACON

richard sharke

CURRENT TIME = FRIDAY, JANUARY 14 12:24 PM
FIRST STARTED = 00.00HRS GMT ON 01ST JANUARY 2005

ID = TC001\LIVE_RELAY\DOGPILELIVESEARCHDATA0000F
ALWAYS VISIBLE AT: HTTP://WWW.AUTOMATEDBEACON.NET

CURRENTLY BROADCASTING ON THE FOLLOWING FREQUENCIES:
NONE

HTTP://WWW.THOMSON-CRAIGHEAD.NET

READ_ME

+ +

10.

Date: 1.05.05 - 1.07.05
From: Jon Thomson <██████████████>, Alexander Galloway
<██████████████>, "t.whid" <██████████████>, Michael Szpakowski
<██████████████>, curt cloninger <██████████████>, ryan griffis
<██████████████>, "M. River" <██████████████>, Rob Myers
<██████████████>
Subject: BEACON

Jon Thomson <██████████████> posted:

BEACON. A new on-line artwork by Thomson & Craighead, 2005.

At 00.00hrs on January 1st 2005 an automated beacon began broadcasting
on the web at:

http://www.automatedbeacon.net

The beacon continuously relays selected live web searches as they are
being made around the world, presenting them back in series and at
regular intervals.

The beacon has been instigated to act as a silent witness: a feedback
loop providing a global snapshot of ourselves to ourselves in
real-time. As resources become available, ŒBeacon_ will also begin
broadcasting an audio version of this signal across the web and as a
series of short wave radio broadcasts and FM local area broadcasts
_time and places to be confirmed. A physical display system is also
being developed for installation in public spaces, galleries &c. Please
make any enquiries to:

info@automatedbeacon.net

best wishes,
Jon & Alison

+ + +

Alexander Galloway <██████████████> replied:

There have been many projects that use real-time displays of random
search strings, here are some:

http://www.metaspy.com/

http://www.google.com/press/zeitgeist.html
http://www.wordtracker.com
http://sp.ask.com/docs/about/jeevesiq.html
http://50.lycos.com/
http://buzz.yahoo.com/
http://search.store.yahoo.com/OT?

How does Beacon differ from these other sites? more specifically, what makes it an artwork?

+ + +

"t.whid" <█████████████> replied:

Hi all,

An oldie but a goodie that seems relevant:

http://www.mteww.com/mtaaRR/news/twhid/google_netartmasterpiece.html

submitted in the spirit of discussion.

+ + +

Michael Szpakowski <█████████████>

Curious to find myself defending, if this is the right
term, a piece like this, which ordinarily would not be
at all to my taste .
It's the massively concentrated *calling attention to*
the linguistic content of the search strings which are
here denuded of their original context - assisted by
the rather splendidly austere design of the page-
which does it for me.
The outcome is genuinely poetic and moving , it seems
to me, and thank god, irreducible to an artist
statement or simple explanation - its something to do
with zeitgeist, yes; also something to do with an
enormous sense of multitude but also something to do
with a linguistic pleasure akin to me to that I derive
from the work of Alan Sondheim, for example.
And that pleasure isn't simply ,abstractly, linguistic
but also refers very directly to the world out there
in a sort of updated automatic writing -but rather
than the outpourings of a single unconscious, we have
access to almost literally a *collective* unconcious.

reasons to hate thomson & craighead

julian stallabrass

Head to the online work, *e-poltergeist*, from Thomson and Craighead's website and you are greeted with the following warning:

> Save whatever you're doing and
> close all other running applications

It is worth paying attention since, once launched, *e-poltergeist* invades the computer, opening dozens of browser windows (many of them advertising pop-ups), which multiply further if you try to shut them down. Faced with that proliferating field of data, you may well be uncertain about what to do. Some forms of interaction continue to work — hyperlinks operate, as does scrolling, so you can still browse the Web. You can even alter the fundamental appearance of the piece by tiling its windows. Yet the subject of this browsing – commerce and the difficulties of listening, or speaking and being heard and understood – is forced on the user, as is the ominous if kitsch soundtrack. The computer has become possessed by the mischievous spirit of the title, the user is put in the position of divining messages from the flow of information overload which pulses or flickers (depending on the speed of machine and connection), and the music provides a sense of narrative flow, glamorising the process of staring, clicking and typing, just as Hollywood treats hackers, straining to invest office tools with high drama. Are users on the edge of an earth-shattering discovery here, as when Neo decides to follow the white rabbit? Of course not; they are surrounded by marketing detritus, of which the soundtrack is an integral part, and Thomson and Craighead's program, which can be halted only by restarting the computer, is a critical mutation of 'push' technology, and more broadly of the ubiquitous effort to force promotional messages on the public, while investing them with the air of drama, significance and narrative force.

e-poltergeist contains many of the components common to Thomson and Craighead's work. It uses found material; it sets the cloyingly sentimental ('Is nobody listening?') against the crassly commercial; it shifts very familiar material and scenarios into an absurd key. Yet it is remarkable that as makers of such mildly disconcerting, outwardly disarming, and even entertaining work, Thomson and Craighead have provoked among art professionals considerable controversy, and even occasionally outright opprobrium. So it is worth asking why this should be, and whether these reactions are symptoms of a deeper unease about digital art that draws on found material, and appears to generate itself.

Thomson and Craighead play with data streams, games, muzak and cutesy animations, and they sell art trivia. From what they mine in the virtual world, they produce novel combinations of, for example, news headlines and screen-saver animation (*Decorative Newsfeeds*) or global weather data and elevator music (*Weather Gauge*), or animated GIFs, click buttons in a modernist grid, online messages and cheesy soundtracks (*Weightless*). These works bring together data laden with emotional import (from expressions of sentiment or obscenity to news photographs) and throw it against the banal milieux of the airport lounge and the online shop. The effect is just different enough from the experience of passing through modern commercial environments to estrange it. In their exploration of popular online culture can be detected an amused condescension at people's behaviour, and a gathering of vulgar sentiment and behaviour tweaked for the entertainment of the art elite. Yet none of this is exceptional of a segment of art world activity — indeed it is largely typical.

If there is something distinct about Thomson and Craighead, it is that they make such light play with their found material. Their tart combinations of elements of mass and popular culture make few concessions to the aesthete. Many artists who deal with such material transform it, say, from toy figurine to full-blown sculpture, or buff and tweak it to flaunt its vulgarity in a fashion that is subtly aesthetic, and in substances that, like bronze, carry with them the freight of durability and esteemed quality. Thomson and Craighead spatchcock elements of pre-existing tat, and rub the noses of art-goers in the tawdry material that they have gone to the gallery to escape. Normally, the decorum of the gallery, and the type of behaviour expected of those present, would in viewers' minds tend to transform even this kitsch into high art. Yet the muzak that Thomson and Craighead often use annihilates detached observation, bearing the viewer from gallery to mall, and ensuring that kitsch remains just that. (It also serves to remind viewers that galleries are more like malls than they may care to imagine.)

More provocative, though, than the content and style of Thomson and Craighead's work is their exploration of alternative art economies. The art work is an unusual type of commodity, protected from the vulgar forces of commercialisation by its rarity or uniqueness, and sold to selected buyers through exclusive agents. The arrangement has long protected art's cultural freedom to distinguish itself from every element of the mass, to the satisfaction of an overlapping cultural and economic elite. This world is under pressure as the number of buyers for contemporary art grows with its increasing popularity, brought about largely by the marketisation of the museum, and because works are increasingly made in reproducible media. It is unclear why, other than for purely business reasons, artists' films should be available only in limited editions, protected even from students who would study them. The tension is most clearly felt in the online realm, which is fundamentally at odds with the art economy, despite efforts to section off areas of it for exclusive commercial purposes. Internet art, being immaterial, can be copied perfectly and distributed for very nearly no cost — and this against a world dependent upon shutting up rare or unique objects in museums and bank vaults. It is hard to control the display of online art or to claim ownership over it. Art sites that have attempted to shut people out or impose membership schemes have had their contents copied to freely available 'mirror' sites. Less dependent upon art institutions, professional curators and corporate sponsorship, a culture has emerged online in which the old borders between art and public, and art and other culture or even political activism, have eroded, and in which there is much collaboration and conversation.

Thomson and Craighead have pushed on these contradictions in their efforts to sell cheap editions out of an online shop, and, in a related development, by exploiting the auto-generative properties of digital media to create a potentially infinite series of unique works. Items sold or given away from their *dot-store* included old tapes of mobile phone conversations scanned using surveillance equipment and sold in sealed Walkmans, tea-towels displaying Google search results of emotive phrases ('Please Help Me', for example), tiny 3-D badges that flicker to display the Mac or PC wait logo, e-cards borrowed from the Net, harmonising mobile phone ring-tones, and a downloadable version of the old computer game, 'Breakout', in which users have to free themselves from an outdated browser to regain the comforts of contemporary computing. These goods, containing, behind the amusement they provoke, a partially submerged critical point, are displayed in an elaborately designed website that unites many of Thomson and Craighead's concerns over their career, particularly the connection between commercial and personal behaviour online. Its cool design, teetering on the cheesy with its metallic sheen, its pop-up windows advertising unlikely goods, its help page which unhelpfully contains appeals for help, parodies the model of online selling. Many of *dot-store's* elements are lifted unaltered from the Web, and their display serves as a primer in online anthropology. Behind the parody, however, there is a genuine attempt to discover whether artists can viably sell their work online, and break with the protected and restricted art market. Thomson and Craighead operate here as a cottage industry, like most artists, but with the huge advantage of built-in means of wide availability and, for the downloadable elements at least, very cheap distribution.

Leaving the arena of contemporary merchandising, other works touch on the opportunities and dangers of automated art. The elements in *Weightless*, for example, were largely lifted from the Web, and if any one juxtaposition of animation, music and text would be as affecting as any other, why not let the machine make the selection? Simple versions of such automation have a fairly long history, but accessible programming tools and the vast database of material that is publicly and readily available on the Web have handed artists a new set of possibilities. Thomson and Craighead have recently launched a 'beacon' that captures text typed into search engines, forming an impromptu poetry, for online display and radio broadcast. *BEACON* uses only one found element; but it raises the question: how complex can such work become?

In *Short Films About Flying*, various online elements are assembled by the computer to form the said films: first, a video-feed from a camera at Logan Airport, Boston which is controlled remotely by web users who track aircraft, pigeons or suspicious persons as fancy takes them; second, intertitles of the kind found in silent movies, selected using a search engine that picks out particular series of words (such as 'he says...' and 'she says...'); and finally, a soundtrack randomly snatched from the online ether. The results are curious, eerie films in which the soundtrack sets a mood, the intertitles often seem to build the beginnings of a narrative and the pixellated video footage, banal though it is, holds out the promise or threat of some impending event. The viewer knows that each film is randomly or near-randomly generated, and questions their urge to find coherent meaning in the conventional association of video images, music and words.

The computer can go on manufacturing these little films without limit, and it is a simple matter to sell them as videotapes through a shop, or make them available free online. Can anyone, then, own a Thomson and Craighead 'original' if they choose to? Not quite, because the authorship of these films is uncertain: the artists set up the framework into which content is poured, and wrote the complex program that assembles the work's elements but they have no control over their precise combination and over the camera's movements.

Online art has typically divided itself into two complementary camps: that which dwells on the commercialisation of the Net, the conquest of its commons by corporations, and the willing participation of many in the online mall experience (to the extent, as Thomson and Craighead point out, of incorporating links to bookstores from memorial pages to their loved ones); and that which seeks to combat the consuming culture with meaningful participation and dialogue. One, then, centred on the current online mall-dystopia; the other on using the technology to empower users in talk and action, and opening on the utopian possibility of an empowered, responsible, debating public — a real democracy.

Yet each division contains a fragment of its other. The dystopian exploration of and intensification in art works of commercial culture casts, as its implicit shadow, the ideal of a genuinely democratic culture; equally, the work which idealistically throws itself against the climate of commercial culture does so in full knowledge of that culture's vast extent and insidious character, and of the subsequent fragility of dialogue's prospects. In the first, technological means are used to highlight the uses made of technology by mass culture; in the second, technological means are used to open spaces against that social reality.

Works that generate themselves, though, do not fit comfortably within either camp. The artists who dwell on dialogue often produce work that is incomplete, or can never be completed, and over which they necessarily surrender control. Thomson and Craighead's auto-generative works marry the polish of the authored, dystopian work with the endless cycle of dialogue. In these works, there may be glimpsed the comfortable critique that much mass culture is manufactured as if by machine (that there is now a computer program capable of grading the chance of songs to make the Top Ten, and which is hired out to record companies, should not be a cause of surprise). Their darker side turns on whether that critique can be extended to the art world – particularly when art works of all kinds seem to be more commonly novel juxtapositions of ready-made objects or elements – or even to the human creative process as a whole.

Computer-generated works are one of the plainest indicators of the pressure that the digital revolution applies to the old forms of ownership, manufacture, pricing and passive consumption. Various threats congeal in this association of machine production and online commerce: there is the nightmare that haunted Greenberg, that kitsch and its vulgar mass audience would simply overwhelm high culture (art's only protection being to hold itself to its own exclusive and essential concerns); there is the linked concern that the mechanical production of culture has the capacity to augment greatly the already strident and ubiquitous power of mass culture; and for the old art world, there is the threat that such products will be linked to a distribution system that can reach anyone online.

At this point, the art professional sees a world crumbling, visions of empty galleries, unique works owned by everyone, a stuttering and then failing of artspeak amid a mass proliferation of 'work' and comment, the autonomy of art ruptured, artists and dealers redundant, in short an economy broken and the sacred polluted with the profane. Naturally, representatives of the old order, more or less sharply aware of dark clouds gathering at their horizons, have good reason to hate Thomson and Craighead.

lists

Alison Craighead
1971 born Aberdeen, Scotland
Jon Thomson
1969 born London, England

SELECTED PUBLICATIONS
Tom Corby (ed.), *Network Art: Practices and Positions*
Rachel Greene, *Internet Art*
Lucy Kimbell (ed.), *New Media Art: Practice and Context in UK, 1994 – 2004*
Christiane Paul, *Digital Art*
Julian Stallabrass, *Internet Art: The Online Clash of Culture and Commerce*

IN COLLECTION
Arts Council Collection: *Triggerhappy*, *Short Films about Flying*

AWARDS
2005   Winners of an Arts Foundation Fellowship
2004   Fellows at The MacDowell Colony, New Hampshire, USA

SELECTED WEB WORK
2005   *BEACON*, www.automatedbeacon.net
2004   *Template Cinema*, www.templatecinema.com
2002   *dot-store*, www.dot-store.com
1998   CNN *Interactive just got more interactive*, www.cnnextra.net
        Weightless, www.thomson-craighead.net/w/
        Triggerhappy, www.triggerhappy.org
1997   *Pet Pages*, www.pet-pages.org
        Attributed text, www.attributed-text.net

FOR MORE INFORMATION
www.thomson-craighead.net

JON THOMSON & ALISON CRAIGHEAD WOULD LIKE TO THANK
Kris Cohen
Sarah Cook
Philip Crean
Luci Eyers
The MacDowell Colony
The Arts Foundation

PICTURE CREDIT
pp46-47: pack shots for *dot-store*, Alan Cook
p53:   installation photograph, Media Lounge, The Media Centre,
          Huddersfield.
p61:   installation photograph, Steve Dietz
p62:   installation photograph, Tamas Banovich